DIGITAL AND INFORMATION LITERACY ™

DESIGNING, BUILDING, AND MAINTAINING
WEBSITES

REVISED AND UPDATED

J. POOLOS

rosen publishing's
rosen
central®

New York

Published in 2018 by The Rosen Publishing Group, Inc.
29 East 21st Street, New York, NY 10010

Library of Congress Cataloging-in-Publication Data

Names: Poolos, Jamie, author.
Title: Designing, building, and maintaining websites / J. Poolos.
Description: New York : Rosen Central, 2018. | Series: Digital and information literacy | Includes bibliographical references and index. | Audience: Grades 5–8.
Identifiers: LCCN 2017023103| ISBN 9781499439014 (library bound) | ISBN 9781499438994 (pbk.) | ISBN 9781499439007 (6 pack)
Subjects: LCSH: Web sites—Design—Juvenile literature.
Classification: LCC TK5105.888 .B3795 2017 | DDC 006.7—dc23
LC record available at https://lccn.loc.gov/2017023103

Manufactured in China

CONTENTS

INTRODUCTION

For a newcomer, the idea of creating a website from scratch can likely seem pretty overwhelming. However, anyone with an Internet connection can build one. Different types of sites requires different know-how, but all web pages and sites require the same basic knowledge.

A single web page can stand on its own, while a website is made up of many such pages. There are many different formats and forms a web presence can take online. A historical website about the Vietnam War hosted by the Public Broadcasting System (PBS) may be devoted to a single topic, for instance. However, it may have many different web pages comprising it, including transcripts, and links with video and other supplemental materials. Moving from one part of a website to another is done via the hyperlinks that usually pop up when you scroll over them with a mouse or a typepad on a computer, or use a touchscreen on a smartphone or tablet.

Web developers are the people that create websites. Most are professionals, but there are many that do it as a hobby, too. All of them must think carefully about what they hope to accomplish when developing a site. From its design, to its construction, and rolling it out for the use of others via publishing, this planning is integral to sites that work properly, look good, and are easy to use.

It is easier to build a website nowadays than ever before. Learning how to do so can lead to a great career and can be an extremely useful skill to have regardless of one's profession.

Web design is important to the look and feel of a site, but it is web developers that control what happens behind the scenes. One can compare the job of a web designer to that of a person who designs what a car might look like on the outside, versus the mechanical engineers and mechanics that concentrate on the parts under the hood that make automobiles run.

There are many factors to consider when creating websites. Beyond good graphic design, the coding provides the instructions that help accomplish what the users of the website need accomplished. Web developers usually need to know several programming languages these days to make good sites, and to make them reliable, efficient, quick, and responsive. They also need to know how to troubleshoot, fixing both standard problems and unexpected ones that may arise.

Many web developers study for years, and truly professional ones are always keeping up with the newest developments. But simple, effective websites are within the grasp of even inexperienced but dedicated students of web development. A few weeks or months of reading and studying can provide a budding young programmer with the basics needed to start out.

Once they do, building websites can be an exciting hobby and, naturally, a very rewarding and lucrative career path. Businesses, individuals, nonprofits, and government agencies all need websites built and maintained. With the Internet now a dominant part of modern life for billions of people worldwide, building web development skills and keeping them sharp will always be assets in high demand.

Chapter 1

Websites: How They Work

When someone turns on their computer or other Internet-enabled device, opens a browser, they usually enter a website address in the appropriate field of the browser. That address can be loaded there. Web addresses also exist as link within the text and imagery of websites themselves. Click on them, or load an address via browsers like Google Chrome, Safari, Firefox, or Internet Explorer.

By taking this action, you are actually summoning the files, code, and display materials of the website, and using them through that browser. If there is some problem, the browser will usually present an error message (for example, if there is no internet connection, or the site has been taken down).

Websites operate on the world wide web. In the most basic sense, the web is a network of information all over the world. It resides on computers called servers that computers all communicate with one another via the internet, allowing billions of people to share information and perform transactions.

Putting together a website for the first time might seem daunting. Turning it into a group project could help make it fun and insightful. Team members can pool their talents and inspire each other in problem solving.

People use websites to share information and exchange text, pictures, videos, audio, and software applications. News organizations like *CNN*, the *Wall Street Journal*, and the *New York Times* publish stories and videos online. Universities offer remote classes, so students can learn from home. Businesses of all kinds sell their products and services online. Individuals publish their ideas on blogs, and create communities, and share news and media via social networks like Facebook, Twitter, and Instagram.

Although billions of people all over the world go online for these and other purposes, it wasn't all that long ago that the concept of surfing the

Internet didn't even exist. Computers sharing signals over a network was not a reality until the 1960s. At this time, the U.S. Department of Defense began work on creating a network of computers. In 1985, an American research organization called the National Science Foundation developed what we know now as the Internet.

As the Internet developed and became easier to use, different parties saw its huge potential. Large corporations, like telecommunications companies, built their own networks. Soon, there were many networks connected to one another. An Englishman named Tim Berners-Lee achieved the first connection linking a server to an Hypertext Transfer Protocol (HTTP) client in 1989. In 1991, the world wide web went live for the first time—initially to researchers, and then to the general public.

Broader Bandwidths

As new technologies are developed to satisfy the needs of consumers, old technologies fade away. Some say that online technologies become outdated within three years' time. This forward march of change can be overwhelming, but also liberating.

During the early part of the Internet era, the gold standard for data transfer was a T-1 line that transfered up to 1.5 megabytes per second. In 2015, the Federal Communications Commission (FCC) declared that the standard for "broadband" was now 25Mbps, from 4Mbps, according to PCMag. Since this was written, average commercial speeds have likely increased even more. Because data can now be sent at a much higher rate, Web developers can create sites with the ability to host ever richer animation and high-definition streaming video, among other capabilities.

Pages, Browsers, and Servers

The Internet is a worldwide system of computer networks through which data travels. The Web can be thought of as the collection of sites, hyperlinks, social networks, and e-commerce sites, among other destinations, that exist on the Internet. The three components that allow the web to function are the web page, the browser, and the server.

A HTML document is a document that is displayed by a web browser. Composed of text, HTML documents include both content and directions that tell the browser how to display the content. For example, the actual web page the user views may display the word "Hello." The HTML document contains this content (the word "Hello") and guidelines for its display—such as it being centered on the page and in 12-point type.

Along with the millions of websites online, and the billions of users that utilize them, there are thousands upon thousands of server rooms worldwide to help host them. A single online session of an hour or two might connect you to dozens of different ones.

A web browser is a software application used to retrieve web pages from web servers and to present them in a form a user can read. Browsers are installed on a user's computer, called a client, as well as on smartphones and tablets.

A web server is both the software that delivers (or serves) web pages when someone requests them, and also the dedicated computers that run these programs. The computers known as servers are not like everyday, personal computers. Instead, they are generally large pieces of hardware are kept in special climate-controlled rooms, on account of the large amounts of heat they generate. Web pages, browsers, and servers all work together over the Internet to make communication possible. This is how the process works:

1. A student sitting at a computer connected to the Internet opens a Web browser, types "http://www.cnn.com" into the browser address field, and presses the return or enter key.
2. The browser connects to the server where the CNN.com home page is stored and requests the page.
3. The server sends the page back to the student's browser. The page is sent as HTML text.
4. The browser reads the HTML, deciphers it, formats the information (including text, pictures, and video), and then displays it on the screen as a Web page that the student can read.

Hypertext Markup Language [HTML]

Before a web page can be stored on a server and served to the student's computer, someone has to create it. Web pages contain directions that tell the browser how to display the content. Those directions are contained in HTML tags. HTML stands for hypertext markup language.

When a person creates a web page in a text editor or an HTML editor, he or she places the HTML code in brackets, called tags. HTML tags tell the browser a number of things, like to display text in a particular color and size. HTML tags also tell the browser to set the text in a

11

User satisfaction is one of the most important goals in mind when someone plans a website. Satisfied visitors will come back to the site again and again.

certain number of columns, or to place a picture in the middle of the page. Here's an example of HTML:

> This text is
> bold.

The "b" within the tags tells the browser to make the text between the tags bold. The sentence looks like this on the web page:

> This text is **bold**.

The tags don't display on the web page. Only the sentence displays, along with the formatting—in this case, the bold typeface.

HTML is the building block for web page authoring, but there are other programming languages that can tell the browser how to display a web page. These include CSS, Flash, Javascript, and XML. These languages are more sophisticated and powerful than HTML, and they allow knowledgeable web page authors to build fast, user-friendly websites.

Chapter 2

Website Planning

Planning is a vital stage in making sure websites are created easily, run how they are supposed to, and allow users to perform the tasks they are designed to do. Good planning can save time, make a developer work more efficiently, and help stay focused on the task at hand. There are several things to consider when planning one's work in creating a site.

What Is the Website For?

The first thing to do when developing a plan is to determine what the goal of the site is. Every website begins with a goal of what a developer hopes to achieve. The goal will determine the direction that the web design takes. Another synonym for "goal" in this context is "purpose." In thinking about this ultimate purpose, one can start big and then work one's way down.

If the intention is to deliver information about horses, for instance, the first thing to consider is exactly what kind of information about horses will the website cover. What about if your site is simply going to provide

E-commerce success means providing online shoppers the easiest possible way to purchase what a site is selling, without making them dig too much.

information and nothing else? It will probably include pictures, text, and maybe videos. A site that is intended mainly to sell books should be designed as an online store. The person designing the site would want it to display the books so potential buyers could view them. The site might also describe the books in detail, clearly state their price, enable customers to buy books with their credit cards or other payment methods, and provide them with a way to check on their orders. Any objectives or features of a potential website that doesn't meet a need of the goal should be discarded.

Who Is the Target Audience?

After the website creator has determined the website's basic needs, it's time to consider the needs of the site's audience. These are the people who the creator believes will want to visit the website. Most members of the audience will have something in common. For example, most potential visitors to a website discussing different kinds of equestrian (horse-riding) competitions will likely have a general interest in horses.

One benefit of establishing this audience allows the website's creator to concentrate on the needs of that audience. He or she can then focus the

Fans of a brand, like the shoppers lined up here at the urban fashion store Supreme in London, England, are an example of an audience or demographic group that a website designer might work to appeal to.

site's content on what will appeal to its target demographic. Of course, many websites will have some characteristics that would appeal to newcomers to a topic or interest.

Research is the best route to determine the target audience. The Internet can provide a number of clues about potential users. For example, a person setting up a website about the Revolutionary War might run a search to identify other sites that discuss the topic. Her or she might talk to classmates and teachers about their interest in this historical era, and determine what they might want to see in a site on the topic. He or she can learn more about the subject by talking to an expert about the revolutionary era to find out what kind of information people typically look for.

File   Edit   View   Favorites   Tools   Help

GATHERING WEB ANALYTICS

Gathering Web Analytics

Web analytics programs gather and analyze web usage data. Web analytics measure website traffic and serve as the basis for user analyses. There are two ways data is gathered. One is by logfile analysis, in which the web server's transactions are counted and analyzed. The second is by tagging, which records the number of times a page is rendered. Together, these measures help individuals and businesses make decisions about their websites. Such measures allow them to make changes that can drive traffic. This includes analyzing times of day with the most and least traffic, or visits, and adjusting accordingly.

Planning a Website's Content

Once a creator identifies their target audience, their next step is to make their site appealing to that audience. Will people visiting the website already have a basic knowledge of the subject involved, or will they need a basic or even thorough explanation of it? It's important to match the content to the target audience's probable expertise and interest level.

It is important to isolate the exact information that the website needs to contain and provide. It can be very helpful to make a list of all of the bits of data, topics, and subtopics. Organizing these in an exact fashion can come later. But deciding on the level of detail the site will provide is vital. Although more detail usually means more work, audiences may benefit from taking this more in-depth approach.

Once the site's content has been determined, it's time to decide how best to deliver the information to the audience. There are many options for

Media	Use	Cost
Text	Text can be used to present complex information, or when a quick verbal explanation is all that is needed.	Text can take up a lot of space. On its own, text is not very flashy.
Photographs	Images enhance a story and can provide information at a glance.	Photographs can be hard to get. In addition, some time is required to manage image files. Too many image files can slow down the website.
Illustrations	Much like photographs, illustrations can enhance a story and provide information at a glance. They can also create a tone and give the site character.	Creating illustrations can be time consuming. Illustrations also have the issues as photographs when it comes to slowing down a website.
Video	Video can tell a story and show real action in a way text can't.	Video can take time to create, process, and load to the Web server. Videos can also slow down the website.

presenting content on the web. Each serves a specific purpose, and each has a cost.

After defining the target audience, creating the content the audience wants or needs, and determining how to deliver the content, its time to begin the process of organizing the content into web pages and designing the actual website.

MYTHS & FACTS

MYTH The more pages and features on a website, the better it is

FACT More pages and features mean more work for the person building the website. Broken links, out of date pages, and unused features don't impress anyone. Clear and simple websites are generally the most effective. Pages and features can be added as they are needed.

MYTH Once a website is built and published, it will immediately be viewed by visitors.

FACT A site can't be visited until someone finds it. Major search engines may not index the site for several months after it is published. Meta tags can be used to draw drive traffic to a site.

MYTH A person needs to be completely fluent in programming languages before building a website.

FACT There are many programs out there that can help anyone design a website. Learning a programming language such as CSS can help make a website more functional and attractive, but it is not a requirement for web design.

Chapter 3

Website Design

A website's design and construction bring together three different aspects. These include how it is structured, how its various pages are laid out, and how users can navigate around it. One of the developer's goals is to ensure that visitors can easily navigate their site. Another is fostering that navigation to help users find the information they need easily, or to be able to accomplish what they hoped to when visiting. If someone visits a website to find out about a concert and purchase tickets to it, that should be something they can easily do in a few quick steps. One must-have is easy-to-read text.

The Structure of a Website

Website users want to access content or accomplish a goal, without any hassle. A site fails in its mission if users get lost or unnecessarily distracted, or cannot figure out which link best serves their needs. Search engine spiders—automated programs that gather website information for search

The last thing a site should be is confusing. This makes it far more likely that users will simply tune out and click elsewhere. Nowadays, high internet speeds and short attention spans make this even more of a possibility.

engines—will also be able to more easily navigate a site, too. This will improve its position and prevalence in web searches.

The simplest way to think about website structure is to imagine levels, called tiers. A website is best organized in three tiers. The home page is Tier 1. It is the page where visitors land when they type in the website's URL into their browsers. Think of it as a gateway to the website. The Tier 2 pages include most of the broad-level content. Each of these pages may link to any number of Tier 3 pages, which include more detailed information.

At this point in the design process, most developers create site map diagrams to show the organization of their websites. A site map diagram is a simple illustration that describing a website's structure:

Notice that three of the five Tier 2 pages link to Tier 3 pages, while "How To Buy a Horse" and "My Horse Blog" do not link to Tier 3 pages. By employing the tiered system of website structure, website designers can build sites that are easy to use.

Tier 1	Home Page				
Tier 2	About Horses	Caring for Horses	How to Buy a Horse	Horse Gallery	My Horse Blog
Tier 3	Equine History Work Horses Recreational Horses Sports	Daily Care Veterinary Care		Gallery One Gallery Two	

Parts of Web Pages

Not only is it important to create a solid website structure for ease of use, it's vital to make web pages easy to read, attractive, and fast. Accomplishing this means logically and thematically arranging the content. Most web pages are constructed with a few common elements. Some of these include:

- **Background**: The background of a web page is what displays behind the text. It can be a plain colored field, a pattern, a photograph, or even animation.
- **Banners**: Banners sit at the top of the page and usually show the website name. They may include illustrations or images.
- **Fonts**: A font is a specific style and size of type within a type family. The fonts Arial and Helvetica work best on most browsers.
- **Footer**: The footer is like the banner, but it appears at the bottom of the page. It usually contains copyright information or contact information.

- **Headings**: Headings are titles that separate one text block from another. They usually display in a darker and larger typeface than the regular body text.
- **Images**: Images can be used to communicate ideas and add color to a page. They are most effective when they are used intelligently with text.
- **Navigation menu**: The navigation menu includes the links to other pages on the website. It usually appears across the top of the page, under the banner, or along the left side of the page.
- **Text Blocks**: Text blocks can be one or more paragraphs of words on the page, and can display in different colors. A page may include multiple text blocks.

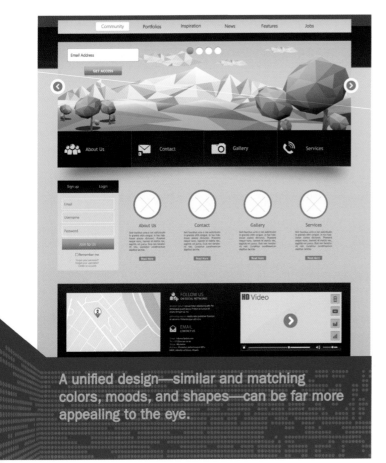

A unified design—similar and matching colors, moods, and shapes—can be far more appealing to the eye.

Web Page Design

All of these elements are usually arranged in columns on the page. (A column is a division of a page from top to bottom.) The most popular layouts use two or three columns. Most pages of a website will have an identical layout. Some pages may require a different design. For instance, a typical information page may use three columns, while a gallery of photographs may use only two columns.

File   Edit   View   Favorites   Tools   Help

STARTING A BLOG: BUILD IT YOURSELF, OR PICK A PLATFORM

Starting a Blog: Build It Yourself or Pick a Platform

For some online activities, things that used to require more complex coding skills are now more streamlined. One of the best examples are blogging platforms. While it is certainly possible to build a website from scratch with your own coding abilities, few people nowadays choose to make the effort. There are dozens of blogging platforms, which might be considered a form of content management system. These include well-known ones like Wordpress and Blogger, and platforms that allow for smaller posts, known as microblogging sites—for example, like Tumblr.

For a young developer, it may be worthwhile to look at some hosted blogs to get ideas, and to try to emulate some of their elements and functions. The point is to build one's skills and sharpen them. Of course, most users that just want to write down their thoughts and broadcast them to online audiences (even just friends and family) would likely employ a hosting service. Most are free, while building a site from scratch often requires fees for hosting and other services

It's important to keep a website's goal, target audience, and content in mind when designing the layout. Web pages with muted colors and uncluttered layouts are often more appealing and easier to read. Thus, avoid densely laid out elements with bright and jarring, or distracting, color schemes.

When using images on a website, it's important to consider how many images will be loaded, as well as their size. Images are loaded from the server and displayed in the browser, just like text. Anyone designing a site should be careful not to use too many images on each page, and to

This screenshot of a page from the NASA website is an example of a website that conveys a great deal of information without too much clutter. The design also conveys a feeling that implies technology and precision.

take care with the image size. This is because images take longer to load from the server than text does. Once an image is loaded, it is stored in the browser's cache. An image can be loaded from the cache more quickly than it can be loaded from the server. Developers take advantage of this and try to use the same image on several pages in order to reduce loading time. For end users (website visitors), many of these factors may not make a huge difference if they have a relatively new computer or device with the most current operating systems and browsers installed. However, the shortcomings of websites that require one's software and hardware to work too hard quickly become obvious on slower systems. Since everyone may have a slightly different system, web developers should try to make it easy for the widest cross-section of users.

Acceptable image formats for use in a website include GIF (graphics interchange format) and JPEG (joint photographic expert group format). GIF files are best for line-art illustrations, like drawings. JPEG files are best for photographs. If an image is in some other format, it must be converted to a GIF or JPEG with an image-processing program. Images must also be sized to fit in the layout and load quickly. If an image is too large, or if the designer doesn't specify its dimensions, the browser can take longer to render it on the page.

A design scheme should be consistent. Banners, backgrounds, colors, fonts, and navigation buttons should have a similar appearance, including matching colors, from page to page. This way, the visitor can feel comfortable with the design and focus on the content.

Chapter 4

Building a Site

The planning stages should yield a good plan or roadmap for the site's construction, including a pleasing design. Now it is time to roll up those sleeves and get down to the nitty-gritty of building the site. Like construction projects in the physical world, this project requires the right tools for the job.

A Good Toolkit

Developers build websites using software applications called tools. These tools make the job of building the website easier and less time consuming. When it comes to building a basic website, only a few tools are needed.

The most important tool a developer uses is an HTML editor. HTML editors allow people designing websites to input HTML code. Many HTML editors also include features that enable people to use dropdown menus to generate the code. With these editors, a user can drag and drop images onto the page, and the editor writes the HTML code that makes it work on the Internet. One of the big advantages of an HTML editor is that a user can use the menus to accomplish a task, and then view the code the editor generates. This is a great way to learn how to code HTML. Some hosting sites allow sub-scribers to use their HTML editors. Popular HTML editors include Adobe CoffeeCup, DreamWeaver, HomeSite, and KompoZer.

Graphics programs are also important tools in web design. They are used to manipulate images, such as photographs. For example, a graphics program can be used to change the dimen-sions of an image so it fits on a web page, or crop images to improve their

Tackling a site from the ground up can sometimes feel like a tough and lonely task, but planning ahead will help.

composition. Popular graphics editors include Adobe Photoshop, Adobe Fireworks, Gimp, and PhotoPlus. Free ones that also allow for creation of web elements include Vectr and SVG-Edit.

In addition to graphics editors, illustration programs enable people to make line drawings and even add colors and patterns to a website. Some people use illustration programs to make cartoons for their sites, or buttons for their navigation menus. Popular illustration tools include Adobe Illustrator, DrawPlus, and Jasc Paint Shop Pro. There are many options developers can shop around for, many of them actually free, or available via trial memberships.

The Home Page and Secondary Pages

Up to this point, someone building a website has a free hand planning and designing the site. However, during the construction of the site, a few strict rules must be followed. The site must be built using well-formed, valid HTML. This means that the website must be coded according to the rules of the World Wide Web Consortium (WC3), which is the governing body that creates web standards. Code that adheres to these standards will work consistently across various browsers and operating systems.

WC3 standards require certain elements on each page. For instance, each page must begin and end with the <html> tag. Each must have a heading as well. A basic page looks something like this:

```
<html>
<head>
<title>The Title Of The Page Goes Here</title>
</head>
<body>
All text, images, and other elements go here.
</body>
</html>
```

The tags, such as <title> and </title>, surround the content and tell the browser how to display it on the screen. There are many different tags available, and they are used for all sorts of purposes, including changing the size and color of text, putting space between paragraphs, and locating elements on a page.

Today, most developers use cascading style sheets (CSS) to define the way the HTML is displayed on the page. The style sheet is a separate file

Avoid getting frustrated if things do not turn out exactly as planned. Good web building can be a process of trial and error. Take as many breaks as necessary to recharge, and then come back refreshed and ready to dive in again.

containing only tags and instructions for display. Each web page refers to this file for display instructions. The advantage of CSS is that a developer can change any style on the website just by editing the style sheet, rather than by editing the HTML of each page of the site.

Website Navigation Menus

Another important design consideration in the construction of a website is the navigation menu. Navigation menus contain the links a visitor clicks on

File   Edit   View   Favorites   Tools   Help

USING META TAGS

Using Meta Tags

Meta tags are HTML codes that are inserted into the header on a web page, after the title tag. They include information about the website. Specifically, meta tags include the meta description tag, which is a statement that describes the site, and meta keywords, which may include any words that may appear in or describe the site. Meta tags do not affect the how the page is displayed, and they are not seen by users. Instead, their main function is to provide meta document data to search engines. When a potential visitor types a key word into a search engine, the search engine looks for the key words in the meta tags of many thousands of pages, returning the results that match best.

to move from one page to another. Because navigation menus are heavily used by visitors to a website, it's important that special care be taken in their design. They should be user-friendly, and sometimes even fun to use.

One basic rule is that the navigation menu display in the same place on every page of the site. Typically, this is horizontally beneath the banner, or vertically on the left side of the page.

On some websites, the navigation menu includes links to each page in the site. Other websites have navigation menus that only link to the next tier of pages. For example, the navigation menu on the home page links to the tier-2 pages, and the navigation menu on each tier-2 page links to the tier-3 pages.

Navigation menus can be simple or dynamic. A simple navigation menu is simply a list of links. A dynamic navigation menu changes when the visitor runs their cursor, arrow, or finger over it with a mouse, typepad, or via

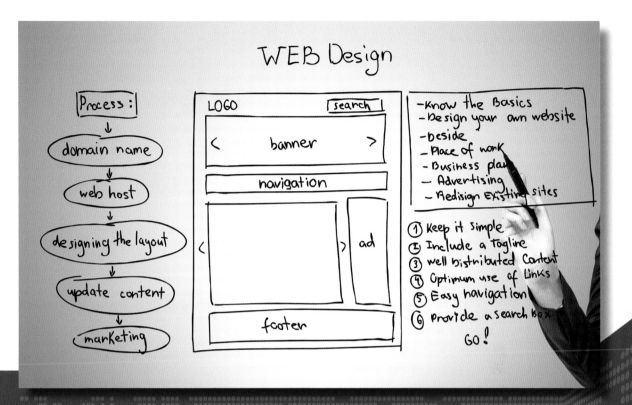

WEB Design

Process:
↓
domain name
↓
web host
↓
designing the layout
↓
update content
↓
marketing

LOGO | search
< banner >
navigation
< > ad
footer

- Know the Basics
- Design your own website
- Deside
- Place of work
- Business plan
- Advertising
- Redisign Existing sites

① Keep it simple
② Include a Tagline
③ well Distributed Content
④ Optimum use of Links
⑤ Easy navigation
⑥ Provide a search box
GO!

Making a visual diagram or plan of attack can help you conceptualize the things that need to be accomplished to build a useful and engaging site. This can be very helpful, especially since much of web developing is so text heavy.

touchscreen. For example, it may at first appear as a list of only the top-level links. When the visitor hovers over one of the links, a short list of sub-links (also called a dropdown menu) appears. The visitor may then click on one of the sub-links to visit the page. Any number of effects may be added to enhance the user experience. For instance, these can include sub menus that fade in or slide down when the mouse hovers over them.

A simple menu is easy to make, loads quickly, and works best for websites with no more than sixteen pages. Dropdown navigation menus take up less space on the page and are more fun to use, but they require scripts, such as JavaScript, to build.

Chapter 5

Publishing and Maintaining a Website

All the code in the world, even if it yields the smoothest-running, most impressive website imaginable, is worthless unless the website makes it online. After building it, the next steps include setting up a domain name for it, and making sure a web hosting service will agree to host it on its servers. Another important task is to test the site, including all the links, and to make sure all elements load and display properly.

Establish a Domain

Acquiring a domain gives a person the right to use a particular URL for their site. Domain names end with suffixes that denote their purpose: .com and .net are used for commercial sites; .org is used by non-profit organizations; and .edu is used by universities.

Domains are usually available through web hosting services, and cost a few dollars a year. The name of the domain usually gives visitors an idea

Web hosting services make use of server farms like this one. Do your homework to find a reliable one that meets your needs and security and privacy criteria. Some hosts are free. For professional websites, paid hosting sevices are usually better.

of what kind of website they're browsing. An individual may choose any name for his or her website's domain, so long as no one else owns the domain.

Find a Web Host

A web host is a service where the files that make up a website are stored. A web host owns and manages the servers that serve the pages to visitors. It rents out

Going live with a site you constructed from the ground up can make for an exhilarating and proud moment. Take pride in a job well done, even as you rededicate yourself to improving and maintaining the site when necessary.

server space to people who want to publish websites. After subscribing to a web hosting service, people can upload the files that make up the website to the host's server when they want to publish the site.

Most hosting services are inexpensive, and some are even free. Each has its advantages and disadvantages, and some are better for certain purposes than others. According to Tizag.com, there are four types of services:

- **Minimal Shared Hosting**: Many websites share a server. Although usually free, this kind of hosting offers few features. For novice web designers, this kind of service can be a great place to start out.
- **Shared Hosting**: Many websites share a server. Although users must pay a small monthly fee, the service is full featured. Shared hosting is mostly used by individuals and small businesses.
- **Unmanaged, Dedicated Server Hosting**: Used by businesses with server administration expertise, this kind of hosting means that a website uses its own server. This enhances security, and the customer conducts all server administration.
- **Managed, Dedicated Server Hosting**: A website uses its own server, but the service conducts all server administration. This kind of hosting is generally used by businesses that want to leave server administration to the pros.

Taking a Site Live

Once the website is finished, a tool called a web validator is used to check for any inconsistencies with W3C standards. The validator looks at the HTML code and shows where any errors appear, so they can easily be found and fixed.

After the site has been validated, it is ready to be published to the server. This is a matter of uploading the website files to the hosting service's computer. When the files have been uploaded, the site is "live." Anyone who knows the URL can type it into his browser and request the web pages.

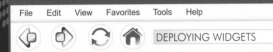

File   Edit   View   Favorites   Tools   Help

DEPLOYING WIDGETS

Deploying Widgets

A widget is a device that is created by a company to perform a function and offered for use on websites and blogs. Literally, a widget is piece of code, called a "snippet," that is embedded in the HTML of a web page. Web designers and bloggers use widgets to make their sites more interesting and informative. For example, there are widgets that display daily weather forecasts, widgets that display slideshows of images, and widgets that can automatically organize blog posts by topic. Many are intuitive, and change a website's appearance and/or potential functions according to inputs that both designers and users provide. There are thousands upon thousands of widgets available.

Once the site is published, it's time for one of the most important tasks: testing. Every page must be checked to make sure it is loading correctly. Every link on every page must also be tested to make sure they work properly, and lead the user where they expect to go. When all of the pages and links check out, the website is finished.

Maintain and Test

Most website designers choose to continually update their sites to keep visitors coming back for fresh content. One important thing to remember is to

Many sites may need to scale up for more users and better functionality. Be ready if it's your site or one made for a friend or even a client. Often, work agreements and contracts for web page work include requirements for following up in case of glitches.

distinguish new content from old visibly. Some webmasters place the date that new content appeared next to its link or headline. That way, visitors can see exactly when that content was added. It obviously helps to list updates or other content chronologically.

In addition to updating the website, testing is a big part of regular maintenance. Web pages and links should be tested periodically. Most importantly, the entire site should be retested any time it is updated. At these times, special attention should be paid to links to other websites, which sometimes change without notice.

TEN GREAT QUESTIONS

TO ASK A WEB DESIGNER

1 Does web design require creativity?

2 How do I get permission to use a particular image?

3 How can I determine if I should build a website or a blog?

4 What programming or development languages should I learn?

5 How often should I update my website, blog, or other site?

6 How can I make the pages of my website load faster?

7 When should I use Flash?

8 How can I track the number of visitors to my site?

9 How do I generate ideas for fresh content?

10 What websites and blogs can help me keep up to date on web design trends?

GLOSSARY

browser A software application for retrieving and presenting information online.

cascading style sheet (CSS) A language used to describe the look and formatting of a document written in HTML.

client A workstation on a network that gains access to central data files, programs, and peripheral devices through a server.

code The symbolic arrangement of statements or instructions in a computer program that allow it to operate.

column A division of a page from top to bottom.

data Information that has been translated into a form that can be processed by computers.

document A computer data file or a web page.

dynamic navigation menu A navigation menu that changes when a visitor hovers over it.

home page The initial page a visitor lands on when they navigate to a website.

hyperlink An object, such as text or an image, that is linked through hypertext to a web page.

internet A worldwide information and data exchange connected via computers, servers, and network infrastructure.

intuitive Direct perception, by sense rather than by reason. In this context, the word describes a navigation system that a visitor may use without having to make conscious decisions.

navigate To move from one page to another on a website (or from one website to another) using hyperlinks.

network A system containing any combination of computers, printers, audio or visual display devices, or telephones interconnected by telecommunication equipment or cables; used to transmit or receive information.

publish In web design, publishing is the act of placing a website on a server and making it available to the public.

security Protection from invasive, unauthorized access to a computer or computer network.

server A computer program that delivers (or serves) content, such as a web page.

site map A diagram that illustrates the structure of a website.

tag A keyword or term assigned to a piece of information on a web page.

tier A layer or level of something.

FOR MORE INFORMATION

International Web Association (IWA)
119 East Union Street, Suite #A
Pasadena, CA 91103
(626) 449-3709
E-mail: Support@iwanet.org
Website: http://iwanet.org
Twitter: @iwanetdotorg
The IWA provides and fosters professional advancement opportunities among
    individuals dedicated to or pursuing a Web career..

Internet Society
1775 Wiehle Avenue, Suite 201
Reston, VA 20190
(703) 439-2120
Website: http://www.internetsociety.org
Twitter: @internetsociety
The Internet Society works to address issues relating to many aspects of
    online infrastructure and culture, including education, standards,
    and policy.

Media Awareness Network
1500 Merivale Road, 3rd Floor
Ottawa, ON K2E6Z5
Canada
(613) 224-7721
Website: http://www.media-awareness.ca.
The Media Awareness Network is dedicated to promoting digital and
    media literacy.

World Organization of Webmasters (WOW)
P.O. Box 584
Washington, IL 61571
(662) 493-2776
Website: https://webprofessionals.org
The World Organization of Webmasters (WOW) is a nonprofit professional
   association dedicated to the support of individuals and organizations
   who create, manage or market web sites.

World Wide Web Consortium (W3C)
77 Massachusetts Avenue
MIT Room 32-G524
Cambridge MA 02139
Website: http://www.w3.org
Twitter: @w3c
The World Wide Web Consortium (W3C) is an international community in
   which organizations, a full-time staff and the public work together to
   develop web standards.

Websites

Due to the changing nature of Internet links, Rosen Publishing has developed an online list of websites related to the subject of this book. This site is updated regularly. Please use this link to access the list:

http://www.rosenlinks.com/DIL/Web

FOR FURTHER READING

Endsley, Kezia. *Website Design* (High-Tech Jobs). New York, NY: Cavendish Square, 2015.

Fontichiaro, Kristin. *Design Thinking*. Ann Arbor, MI: Cherry Lake Publishing, 2015.

Frey, Tara. *Blogging for Bliss: Crafting Your Own Online Journal: A Guide for Crafters, Artists & Creatives of all Kinds*. New York, NY: Lark Books, 2009.

Gifford, Clive. *Computer Networks* (Get Connected to Digital Literacy). New York, NY: Crabtree Publishing, 2015.

Greek, Joe. *A Career in Computer Graphics and Design* (Essential Careers). New York, NY: Rosen Publishing, 2015.

Jenkins, Sue. *Web Design For Dummies*. Indianapolis, IN: For Dummies, 2009.

Lopuck, Lisa. *Web Design for Dummies*, 3rd ed. Hoboken, NJ: John Wiley & Sons, 2012.

Miller, Michael. *Absolute Beginner's Guide to Computer Basics*. Indianapolis, IN: Que, 2009.

Rickaby, Greg. *Creating a Web Site* (Dummies Jr.). Hoboken, NJ: John Wiley & Sons, 2017.

Robbins, Jennifer Niederst. *Learning Web Design: A Beginner's Guide to HTML, CSS, JavaScript, and Web Graphics*, 4th ed. Sebastopol, CA: O'Reilly Media, 2012.

Sabin-Wilson, Lisa. *WordPress for Dummies*. Hoboken, NJ: Wiley, John & Sons, 2009.

BIBLIOGRAPHY

Brain, Marshall. "How Web Servers Work." How Stuff Works. Retrieved September 17, 2009. http://computer.howstuffworks.com/web-server1.htm. http://computer.howstuffworks.com/Web -server1.htm.

Build website 4U. "Website Structure." Retrieved October 21, 2009. http://www.buildwebsite4u.com/building/structure.shtml.

Connolly, Dan. "A Little History of the World Wide Web." Retrieved October 6, 2009. http://www.w3.org/History.html.

Cooper, Charles. "Web 2.0: Obsolete within Three Years?" CNET News, April 23, 2008. Retrieved October 6, 2009. http://news.cnet.com/8301-10787_3-9927521-60.html.

Google.com. "Google Analytics IQ Lessons." Retrieved November 9, 2009. http://www.google.com/support/. conversionuniversity/?hl=en.

Irby, Lisa. "How to Plan a Website." Retrieved October 8, 2009. http://www.2planawebsite.com.

Lissa Explains It All. "Basics." Retrieved October 6, 2009. http://www.lissaexplains.com/index.shtml.

Lissa Explains It All. "CSS." Retrieved November 9, 2009. http://www.lissaexplains.com/index.shtml.

Lissa Explains It All. "Tools." Retrieved October 23, 2009. http://www.lissaexplains.com/tools.shtml.

Olsen, Eric. "Dan Gillmore Interview: SOTB 2009." Technorati.com, October 22, 2009. http://technorati.com/blogging/article/dan-gillmor-interview-sotb-2009.

Rickaby, Greg. Creating a Web Site (Dummies Jr.). Hoboken, NJ: John Wiley & Sons, 2017.

Sethi, Maneesh. *Web Design for Teens*. Boston, MA. Thomson Course
    Technology PTR, 2005.
Tizag.com. "Web Host Types." Retrieved October 6, 2009. http://www.tizag
    .com/webhost/host_types.php.
W3schools.com. "What Is the WWW?" Retrieved October 6, 2009. http://
    www.w3schools.com/web/web_www.asp" http://www.w3schools.com
    /Web /Web _www.asp.
Watrall, Ethan, and Jeff Siarto. *Head First Web Design*. Sebastopol, CA:
    O'Reilly Media, 2008.

INDEX

About the Author

As a technical writer and editor, J. Poolos has been helping people of all ages use computer software for eighteen years. He has designed and developed websites professionally, and he has authored several books for young adults.

Photo Credits

Cover and pp. 1 (far left), 8, 37 goodluz/Shutterstock.com; cover and pp. 1 (center left, center right, far right), 5 Rawpixel.com/Shutterstock.com; p. 10 senticus/Shutterstock.com; p. 12 © iStockphoto.com/track5; p. 14 pixelfit/E+/Getty Images; p. 15 Mike Kemp/In Pictures/Getty Images; p. 20 Olena Zaskochenko/Shutterstock.com; p. 22 Droidworker/ Shutterstock.com; p. 27 © iStockphoto.com/Alexandra Draghici; p. 29 © iStockphoto.com/Marina_Ph; p. 31 ImageFlow/Shutterstock.com; p. 33 baranozdemir/Vetta/Getty Images; p. 37 © iStockphoto.com/ scyther5; cover and interior pages (pixels) © iStockphoto.com/suprun.

Design: Nicole Russo-Duca; Layout: Raúl Rodriguez; Editor: Phil Wolny; Photo Research: Karen Huang